The Orchard Keeper

The Orchard Keeper

Susan Connolly

Shearsman Books

First published in the United Kingdom in 2017 by
Shearsman Books
50 Westons Hill Drive
Emersons Green
BRISTOL
BS16 7DF

Shearsman Books Ltd Registered Office
30–31 St. James Place, Mangotsfield, Bristol BS16 9JB
(this address not for correspondence)

www.shearsman.com

ISBN 978-1-84861-560-1

Acknowledgements
Thanks are due to the editors of the following publications
in which these poems first appeared:

Poetry Ireland Review 106 : 'Matty McGoona's Cottage, Donaghmore,
Navan', 'Cycling to Renvyle'
Boyne Berries 2 : 'Francis Ledwidge'
Boyne Berries 10 : 'At Ellie Vaughey's Grave, Hill of Slane'
THE SHOp 42 : 'Ypres, July 1917'
Reflections on the 1916 Rising, Old Drogheda Society :
'Francis Ledwidge Home on Leave, May 1916'
Cyphers 74 : 'Mornington'
Burning Bush 2 : 'The Beacons at Mornington'
Southword 26 : 'Woman in a Black Hat'
The Stony Thursday Book 14 : 'The Wine-Fountain'

Contents

for
Fiona, Stephen, Rosemary and Tim

The Orchard Keeper

Francis Ledwidge

A five-acre garden, apples, cherries,
Sunday crowds at ease.
Children laughing, blackbirds
sleeping, cherry-drunk.

Matty's fiddle calms you,
your thoughts read at a glance.
You walk the tangled roads
round Slane, dreaming of Ellie.

Homesick in Gallipoli.
Home-rivers wonder where you are.
Killed by shrapnel at Ypres.
Empty roads are grieving.

Matty's grave at Donaghmore,
Ellie's, on the Hill of Slane.
At Rossnaree I saw you,
sleeping by the Boyne.

At Ellie Vaughey's Grave, Hill of Slane

Ellen O'Neill, died July 1915

Ellen, we know you better
as Ellie Vaughey, Frank Ledwidge's
girl; all his poems for you
in autumn nineteen-twelve.

Mondays, on your way to work
at Power's Drapery, Shop Street,
you handed in his 'latest'
to the Drogheda Independent.

But then you married another.
Ellie Vaughey got married!
Frank wrote. *That was a great blow,
perhaps the greatest of all.*

One night at Basingstoke
he dreamed of white birds
flying over the Atlantic ocean,
woke to hear that you had died.

Your brothers brought you home,
and Rita, your infant daughter.
No mention of Francis Ledwidge,
who loved you.

Below the Abbey bell tower
seen from miles away,
dark branches sway
over your grave.

Matty McGoona's Cottage, Donaghmore, Navan

*Christ! Matty it's hard thinking on the old times. The pleasant Sundays
we used to spend and the hopes we entertained!*
    —in a letter from Francis Ledwidge to his friend Matty McGoona

1.

Late September, the smell of ripe
apples filling this overgrown
orchard where six horses graze
near moss-covered cherry trees,
I slip into another century
where you, Matty McGoona,
sit talking for hours with Frank.

2.

Or, nature-noting by the Boyne
at Swynnerton, you return home
at bedtime when Frank relaxes
on his favourite seat near the fire
and you describe stars and spiders,
then listen closely to his poems
all night in the warm kitchen.

3.

I see you thoughtful in your doorway
(your rusty bicycle in a nearby ditch),
reading the last letter Frank wrote you

before leaving for the war:
How is the violin? Every time you play
'The Blackbird' *think on me. I love that tune*
and snatches of it sing in my memory.

4.

He carried that tune across Europe,
until at Boesinghe, near Ypres, he died.
Later, when you played 'The Blackbird'
you remembered Francis Ledwidge
calling to your door with a poem,
the two of you deep in talk, both still safe
from the harm brought by war.

Francis Ledwidge Home on Leave, May 1916

You walked the village roads in May,
those poems for Ellie
like crows flapping darkly around you.

Adrift in drink at the Conyngham Arms
          Hotel.

Sackville Street a smouldering ruin,
you mingled with the crowds,
your British uniform hiding your
         despair.

Summer and autumn in Derry,
you wrote in a room away
from Barracks.
     Words bloomed,
the typed pages gathering
like newly fallen leaves.

The Easter Rising had left you alone,
and all your *dream companions gone.*

Ypres, July 1917

Francis Ledwidge thinks about home

Currabwee and Crewbawn
wait like deer under a tree.
Beauparc and Stanley Hill
listen for my footsteps.

Slug, snail and beetle
creep, birds asleep
in the back garden
at Janeville.

And I can see the way
that dark pine tree
on the Hill of Slane marks
Ellie Vaughey's grave.

The Orchard Keeper

met by chance at Donaghmore, near Navan, Co. Meath

Pushing open the rusty gate,
    all roads narrow to this track
        and a cottage
where I look in a broken window –
    then startled, turn to face
        an elderly man.
When he sees I mean no harm,
    we talk. He shows me the orchard
        round the back,
'where Francis Ledwidge
    wrote his poems,'
        he says.

Sundays in the cherry season,
    the McGoona children
        left cabbage leaves
laden with cherries on the grass.
    Locals spent the evening
        here in conversation.
They ate cherries and played cards,
    blackbirds at ease
        in their company.
Matty's fiddle music filled the air.
    Wasps crawled drunk
        on cherry wine.

I think of Francis Ledwidge,
    of Matty McGoona
        and Ellie Vaughey,

young friends who sat here
in 1912, talking as if nothing
would ever change.
Ellie was the first to die,
then Frank.
Matty lies near
where he grew up, among family
and friends in the graveyard
at Donaghmore.

Woman in a Black Hat

Woman in a Black Hat

for Alison Kelly (1960–2013)

1.

One night she dreamed that a ghostly shape
    stood like a cold breeze
    at her bed
and told her in a rasping voice
    about a part of her life
    she doesn't remember.
Was it lying? Was it telling the truth?
    Could it really know?
Every time she thought about it,
    a shiver rippled
    through her body.

One day she cycled out to the country;
    after a while
    she stopped,
climbed off her bike and stood
    looking quietly
    at the fields.
Not used to such silence
    surrounding her –
she felt it like an arm reaching right
    into her own silence,
    agitating her depths.

Mostly she prefers to put on her black hat
    in the afternoon,

and head for town.
Sitting by herself in the Moorland Café,
    happy in the company
    of strangers –
their bright butterflies of conversation
    drift near her,
distracting her from the emptiness
    felt so often
    at this time of day.

2.

She hears outside her window
    the pawing of things
that need no sleep –
    moonlight and
    creaking branches,
and she understands
what it's like to be like these –
    to be more air and fire
    than earth; so for a while
she's restless, wide-awake –
    younger than a child
    could ever be.

When she's awake
    she has the energy
of elemental things –
    moonlight and
    creaking branches,
but when she sleeps
and her thoughts
    flow freely,
    she sleeps
a deep human sleep.

Cycling to Renvyle

1.

Wheeling their bikes
        uphill from Leenane,
his tancoloured saddlebags
        slung across his carrier,
an old army rucksack
        scraping her back:
cycling all day
        from Westport
to Renvyle,
        stopping to look
at everything.
        In the evening
they freewheel
        from Tully Cross
        down to the sea.

2.

Driving by Lough Muck
        a generation later,
we still feel how a dip
        in the road
carried us half-way up
        the next hill.
At Renvyle memories rush in like waves.
        Leave them there.
Don't say if they had children.
        or where they lived.
They only half-knew
        how happy they were –
ghost-selves
        cycling that road
        forever.

Mornington

Past all the bright
new houses,
down the last
wild road,
we stand on
mussel shells,
watch beacon
lights flash
green, red.

High tide,
the pilot boat,
ships crossing
the sand-bar;
stars shine
their promise
on our lives.

The Beacons at Mornington

Come back, come back
to walk this road,
the wind slack,

river a mirror,
the pilot boat
gone out to sea.

Watch
the beacon lights,
as if somewhere

deep within,
you and I
depend on them.

The pilot boat
returns, guiding
a ship majestic

in the dark –
that's the moment
our lives join,

yours and mine:
the beacons
guide us too.

We watch,
silent as a ship
entering the river.

Mother's Lonely Moments

One November evening
while you and Dad were at Mass,
a thief ransacked your house,
stole cash and all your jewellery.

The morning Dad fell downstairs
with the breakfast tray, delph broken,
a mess of milk, tea leaves, marmalade –
you cleared it up alone.

Your last ever pilgrimage to Knock,
Dad vague, you at the wheel,
your eyes suddenly old, strained
against the rain-blurred windscreen.

The exact moment Dad died,
unforgettable, 11 o'clock Friday morning,
St. Patrick's Day – the first time
I saw you crumple and cry.

That day, your last at home,
your turn to be vague, ours to mind you,
that was the day we took you away,
never a lonelier moment.

The day you died, Tuesday evening,
the roof finally caving in:
from five different places on this earth
your children looked up at the stars.

The Wine-Fountain

Do you remember walking the main street out of Estella? It was evening and we walked lightly, our backpacks left behind at the city hostel. We followed the scallop shell sign marking the way. We were going to the wine-fountain to satisfy our curiosity: was there really red wine on tap?

We stopped at an Avia garage and you bought a litre carton of Sangria. You asked the assistant for two glasses and we drank it fast, then walked alongside the dual carriageway and up a hill until we came to the fountain: *Fuente del Vino*. Red wine on tap but set at drip. All the same, we managed to fill a plastic bottle.

We set off downhill back to Estella. We rose early the next morning, the half-bottle of wine in my backpack like an eye observing the warm day unfolding. At 7 a.m. we passed the wine-fountain again. Walking across a desert landscape on our way to Los Arcos we heard loud music coming from a speck in the distance. As we drew closer and the music got louder, we saw a mobile café and people sitting around on benches under sunshades. *'Cinco kilómetros Los Arcos,'* the café man said. I see us still, mother and daughter, on foot across Spain.

Weeks later, poring over a map, I realised we hadn't walked far. But there in the hot sun, empty of thought and minds set free, it felt like we were crossing the wide world.

Biography

Susan Connolly lives in Drogheda, Co. Louth. Her first full-length collection, *For the Stranger*, was published by Dedalus Press in 1993. She was awarded the Patrick and Katherine Kavanagh Fellowship in Poetry in 2001. In the same year she received a Publications Grant from the Heritage Council of Ireland for *A Salmon in the Pool*, a literary and place-names map of the river Boyne from source to sea.

Collaborations with writer and photographer Anne-Marie Moroney include *Race to the Sea* (1999), *Ogham: Ancestors Remembered in Stone* (2000) and *Winterlight* (2002). With Anne-Marie Moroney she co-authored *Stone and Tree Sheltering Water* (1998), an exploration of sacred and secular wells in Co. Louth.

Her poems have been published in journals and magazines throughout Ireland and the U.K. and are included in the *Field Day Anthology*, Vol IV, *Voices and Poetry of Ireland* and *Windharp: Poems of Ireland since 1916*. Some of her work has been broadcast on The Poetry Programme RTE Radio 1. Susan Connolly's second collection *Forest Music* was published by Shearsman Books in 2009. Shearsman also published her chapbook, *The Sun-Artist: a book of pattern poems*, in 2013.

Bridge of the Ford, her collection of thirty-three visual poems, was published by Shearsman Books in 2016.